CW00404342

The Danish Dream.

The lights in Rubjerg Knude Light House in Vendsyssel were lit up for the first time on December 27, 1900. During the period 1910-1920 great amounts of glacial wash sands deposited in the bluff during the ice age, blew up into the area between the light house and the sea. It was deposited around the buildings, filled the well, and destroyed the gardens. The ravages of the sand and the development of technology made the light house obsolete, and it was finally closed in 1968.

The cliffs of Møn are known for keeping the light green colors of the beech trees all summer long. This is because the large content of lime in the ground makes it difficult for the plants to absorb iron and manganese which they need to form the green color of the leaves. The layers of chalk which form the cliffs in these woods were formed during the Cretaceous period 75 million years ago.

With hoe, shovel, and spade...

Already before the last ice age there were people living here. First hunters and gatherers who were not settled, and who made their tools from rocks and clay. The remains from the oldest known *Dane* – a woman found in a bog in central Funen. She lived around 8,000 B.C., and ate plants and meats. The people began to till the earth, keep animals and use metal implements. It was a custom to bury the dead in burial mounds, and here rich findings of jewelry, weapons and tools have been made. Human sacrifice may have occurred as well. During the 1950s a gruesome discovery was made in Tollund by Silkeborg: A hanged man had been laid down into the bog, where he was preserved for posterity. His last meal consisted of a gruel made from grains and weed seeds.

Pre-Viking figure.

The Tollund man is probably the best kept human from antiquity which has been found anywhere in the world. He lived during the early Iron Age, and died 300 to 400 years B.C., right after the Bronze Age had ended. The Tollund Man was found on 6th May, 1950 in a bog by Bjældskovdal.

A Celtic warrior and a Viking warrior.

The first coins in Scandinavia were minted at Hedeby during the beginning of the 800s. The coins were only struck on one side, and are similar to Frankish coins.

The Gundestrup bowl, also called the Gundestrup kettle is from around year one. Some think the motives are Celtic and that the bowl is from Gaul, but findings in Thrace suggest that the bowl may have been made there. It was possibly the Cimbers who brought the bowl to Jutland, since it is known that they gave the Roman Emperor a similar bowl, and that they had been by Romania.

The Vikings are coming!

Not everyone tilled the soil. In a bog on Als a 40' long boat has been found full of spears, armor, iron swords, and shields, and bears witness to the existence of a strong warrior class. Strong fences were built around the towns to guard against enemies. From around 800 AD and during the following 200-300 years the Danes began sailing off to plunder foreign lands. The Vikings also conquered land and set up trading posts. They went to Greenland, Iceland, The Faroe Islands, Newfoundland, England and Ireland, while their own areas were fortified with the Dannevirke line in Slesvig and forts with earthen ramparts on the islands and in Jutland and Skåne. Many beautiful artifacts have been found from the Viking Age, and we have written sources which describe the customs and beliefs in Odin and Thor and other gods.

The Thunder God and the God of Love, Thor was one of the most popular gods in the Norse pantheon. Much jewelry made during Viking times has the shape of his hammer, Mjolnir.

King Harold Bluetooth's coins.

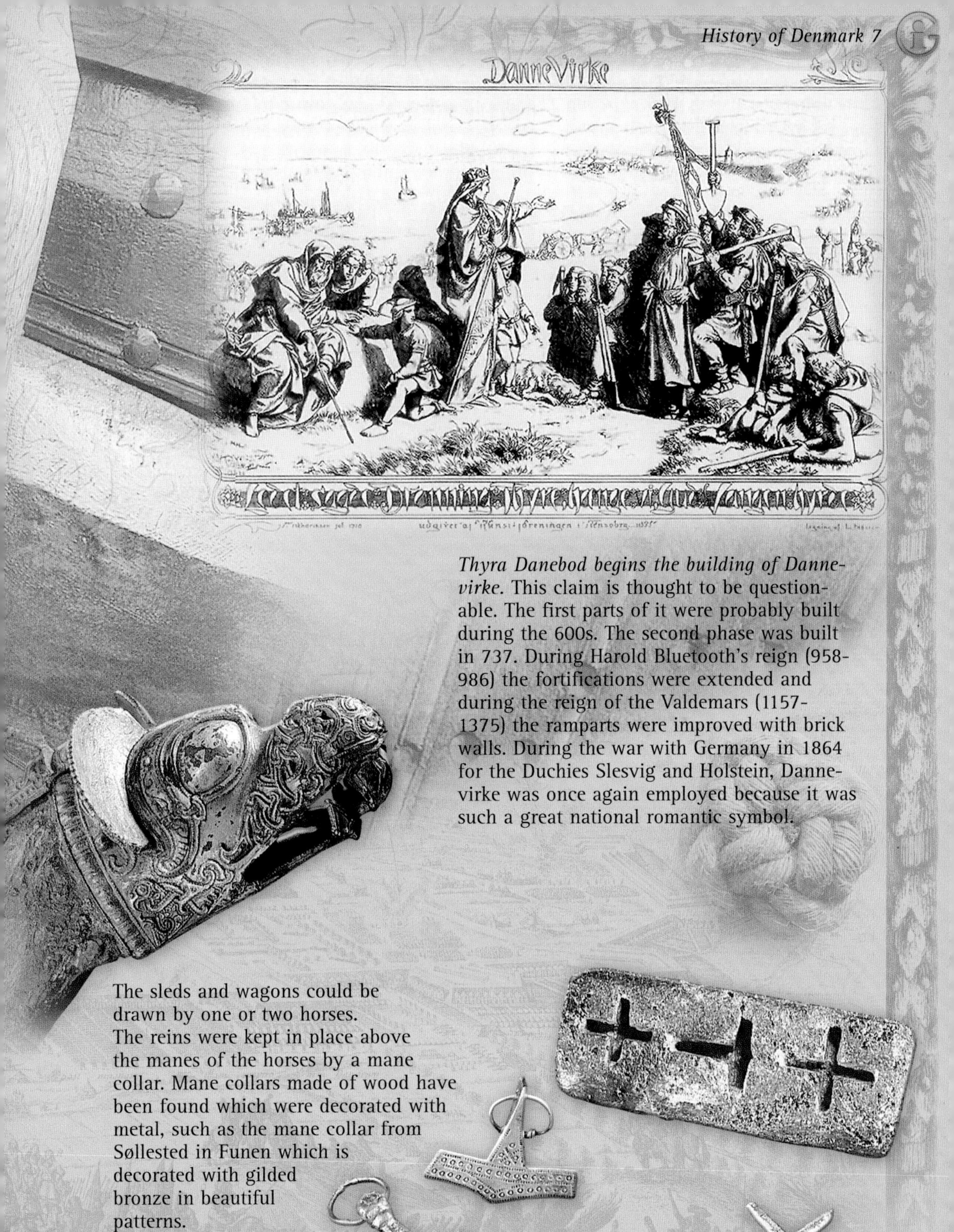

Thyra Danebod begins the building of Dannevirke. This claim is thought to be questionable. The first parts of it were probably built during the 600s. The second phase was built in 737. During Harold Bluetooth's reign (958-986) the fortifications were extended and during the reign of the Valdemars (1157-1375) the ramparts were improved with brick walls. During the war with Germany in 1864 for the Duchies Slesvig and Holstein, Dannevirke was once again employed because it was such a great national romantic symbol.

The sleds and wagons could be drawn by one or two horses. The reins were kept in place above the manes of the horses by a mane collar. Mane collars made of wood have been found which were decorated with metal, such as the mane collar from Søllested in Funen which is decorated with gilded bronze in beautiful patterns.

Die with two crosses and a Thor's hammer.

World Power and Lilliput

When it is appropriate to speak of an actual 'Denmark' is not known with certainty, but the great Jelling Stone which Harold Bluetooth erected in memory of 'Gorm, his father and Thyra, his mother' claims that he 'won' the whole of Denmark. Since then the country has expanded and shrunk several times. Today Denmark is a small country, but it has been smaller still. After the war in 1864 Denmark lost southern Jutland, though it was made Danish again after the First World War. Denmark also ruled over England, and parts of northern Germany and the now Swedish province Skåne have been Danish for long periods of time. During the reign of Margrete I Denmark, Norway, and Sweden were ruled as one.

The Kalmar Union established in 1397.

Arabic coins found in a Viking grave.

Canute II, the Great was described as a man of quick temper but equally quick to regret his actions. He caused churches to be built as a penance for the murders he committed, among them the murder of the Archbishop of Canterbury in 1012 when the bishop had refused to make his poor flock pay the Danegeld.

The night of 1st of February 1864 the Prussians crossed the Ejder Creek with a numerically superior force. Denmark bravely resisted the crushing power of the Prussians, but in vain. Denmark had to cede Slesvig, Holstein, and Lauenburg.

Canute II, the Great's coin.

A reconstruction of the great Jelling Stone which has been called Denmark's birth certificate. The runes along the bottom of the stone say:
King Harold asked to have these monuments made in memory of his father Gorm, and his mother Thyra – the Harold who won all of Denmark and Norway, and Christened the Danes.

The Monarchy

Gorm the Old is considered the first king of Denmark. He was king until the year 958, and since then the country has been governed by a great number of men and two women, our current Queen Margrethe II, and Margrete I whose title was 'Lady and Husband and the Fully Empowered Guardian of the Country'. From 1448 until 1972 Denmark has been governed by a succession of King Christians and Frederiks, aside from a single King Hans. From time to time there was a struggle for the throne. Frederik I banished his nephew Christian II from the throne and it has happened more than once that a king has been murdered. The murder of King Erik Klipping in Finderup Barn is one of the great criminal cases in Denmark's history. One of the best known Danish kings is Christian IV who built the Round Tower, the Stock Exchange, and Nyboder in Copenhagen, and these buildings still stand.

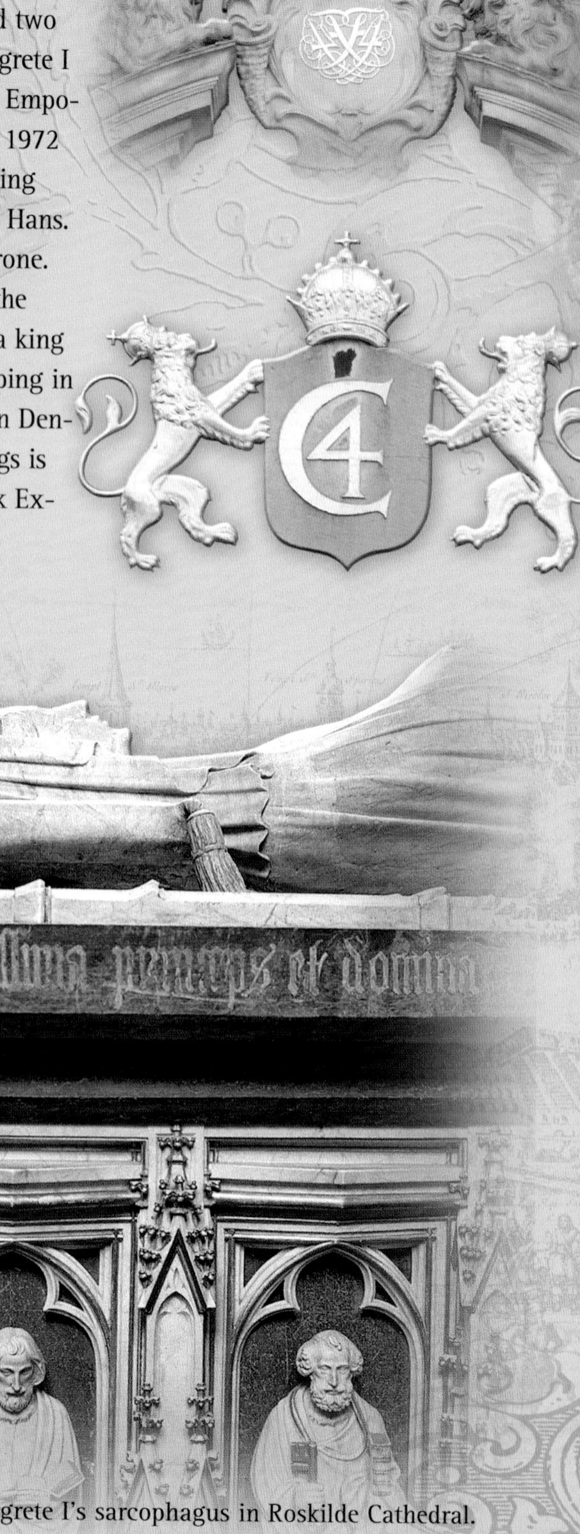

Margrete I's sarcophagus in Roskilde Cathedral.

Kronborg Castle. In the foreground is seen the training ship Dannebrog.

Christian IX marries his daughter Alexandra to the Prince of Wales, Queen Victoria's son, Edward Albert. Later the bride was said to be the most beautiful queen in all of Europe. When King Edward was dying, Alexandra invited his latest mistress Alice Keppel (great-grandmother to Camilla Parker-Bowles) to his death bed.

The Monarchy in Danger

For a little longer than 200 years the Danish kings ruled by despotism. This was not always for the best, such as when a king was mentally ill. This was the case with Christian VII, during whose reign his doctor Struensee managed to take control over the country. The king had such faith in his doctor that he signed all papers which Struensee put before him. The king eventually signed a document saying that the king's signature was no longer necessary, but then Struensee was executed and put on the wheel.

Coronation of Christian VII.

IUSTICE-RAAD STRUENSEE i Flor.
I Preussen var jeg æret Mand,
Min Lærdom höyt mig bragte,
I dette vel behersket Land
Ieg Lykkens Frugter smagte,
Indtil jeg, ved min Broders Raad,
Kom hid til Danmarks Riige
hielpe Ham i Raad og Daad,
Ved Ham til Ære stiige.
derfor paa Hands Fordeel bör
I alle Anslag tænke
ds Dem Sig mod Os sætte tör!
ligt bör os intet krænke.

Struensee's vision encompassed a more enlightened government and greater freedom for the individuals. Here he receives a hopeful representative from the peasantry.

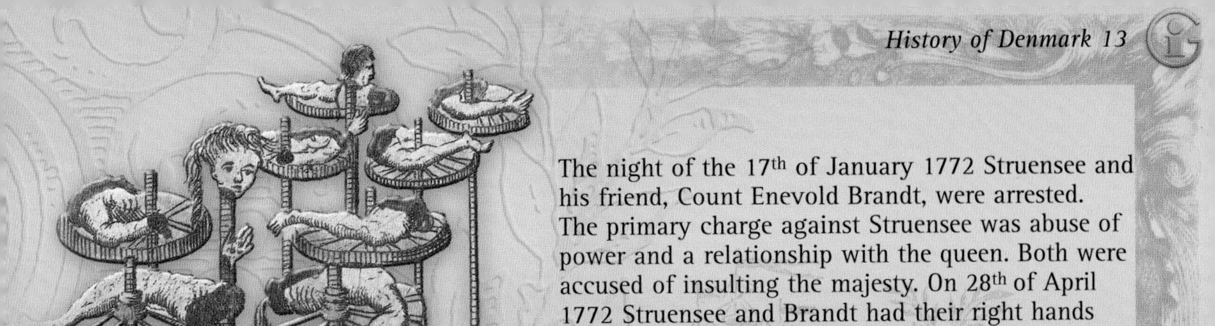

The night of the 17th of January 1772 Struensee and his friend, Count Enevold Brandt, were arrested. The primary charge against Struensee was abuse of power and a relationship with the queen. Both were accused of insulting the majesty. On 28th of April 1772 Struensee and Brandt had their right hands chopped off, and shortly thereafter the executioner was to hold up their chopped off heads before the assembled masses.

In 1848 Frederik VII agreed that the country should have a government by the people and with a constitution, since revolution was around the corner. It is reported that Frederik VII said: *Now I guess I can sleep as long as I please* after he had agreed to abolish despotism.

Frederik VII's equestrian statue in front of Christiansborg Castle.

Frederik VII.

History of the church

te leua
ui animam
meam. de
meus in te
cōfido non
erubescam
neqʒ irrid
ant me

In the middle of the 10th century Harold Bluetooth wrote on the great Jelling Stone that he christened the Danes. This statement ought to be taken with a grain of salt, but it is a fact that the king let himself be baptized and had a church built in Jelling. More churches and a number of monasteries followed. The church also owned castles, among them the impressive fortification Hammershus on Bornholm.

Many of the writings we have from the Middle Ages were written by monks and nuns, among them Saxo's History of the Danes. Most of the writings, among them the Bible were in Latin, but after the Reformation it became possible to read the Bible in Danish. A number of the monasteries and religious artifacts were destroyed during the Reformation. This included the church frescoes, but in Fanefjord Church on Møn the beautiful paintings can still be seen.

In 1486 the printer Stephan Arndes in Slesvig published *Missale Slesvicense*. It is considered the greatest achievement of Danish lithography. It is a beautiful folio, printed in black and red. The elegant Gothic type has an Italian character, and the large initials are hand drawn.

The two Jelling Stones besides Jelling Church. The inscription on the smaller stone says:
kurmr kunukr karthi kubl thusi aft thurui kunu sina tanmakar but
which means: *Gorm King made these monuments after Thyra his wife, Denmark's pride.*

Hammershus is the largest castle ruin in northern Europe. The castle was built in the beginning of the 13th century. Control shifted between the Archbishop in Lund, the Hanseatic town of Lübeck, and the Danish king. In the course of almost 500 years the castle was used as fortress, depot, administration seat for the island and state prison.

According to the legend Saint George saved a town from a dragon which ate sheep and, in lack of sheep, virgins. Saint George arrived when the dragon was about to eat a princess. With a single thrust by his lance he killed the dragon and as a reward the king gave him a large sum of money. George gave the money to the poor of the town before he rode into the sunset. In this wood carving from the 15th century in Roskilde Cathedral, the elements from the Viking Age are still obvious.

Østerlars Church from the 12th century is the best known and largest of Bornholm's four round churches. The church is a central part of the theory about the French Knight Templars and the placement of Bornholm's medieval churches.

The Wars ...

Denmark has participated in many wars. One of the more spectacular took place during the ice winter of 1658, when the Swedish army marched over the ice from Jutland to Funen, across Langeland and Falster to Zealand and finally stood only 20 km from Copenhagen. Upon the armistice Denmark had to cede Skåne.

During a later war Copenhagen was not spared. In 1807 the British let bombs hail down over the city. 1600 inhabitants were killed, and Denmark had to turn the fleet over to England. An eye witness: *Suddenly a bomb fell in Scheuermann's house, and Mouriers came running down to us with great fear. We were now 18 people in Mrs. Falbe's bedroom.*

When Denmark shortly afterwards allied itself with France during the Napoleonic Wars, it resulted in the loss of Norway. In 1848 and 1864 Denmark was at war again, and after the lost war of 1864 Denmark had to cede South Jutland. Since that time there have been no more major battles on Danish soil.

The bombardement of Copenhagen in 1807. The British put a siege on Copenhagen on 16th of August; since there was concern that the crown prince Frederik would turn the Danish fleet over to their arch enemy, the French.

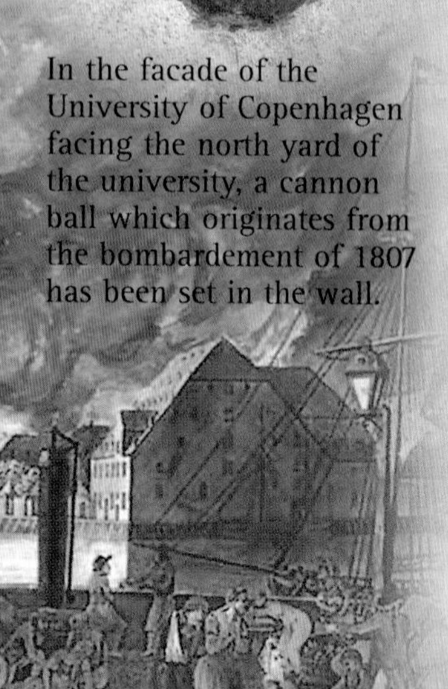

In the facade of the University of Copenhagen facing the north yard of the university, a cannon ball which originates from the bombardement of 1807 has been set in the wall.

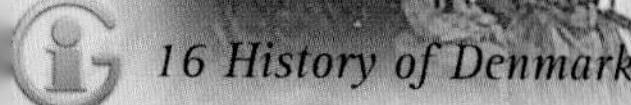

After the German defeat in 1918 the German government accepted that the borders should be rearranged based on the principle of 'the peoples' self determination'. The separation of North Slesvig became the source of much disagreement and division among the Danish minded inhabitants in Slesvig and Danes from the kingdom. Here are Danish election posters from before the election.

Dannebrog falling down from the skies ... from an airplane. The year is 1920 – Reunion feast in South Jutland.

Denmark got in the middle in the war between France and England. On 2nd of April 1801 the British attacked the Danish fleet in the roadstead of Copenhagen. When Admiral Hyde Parker tried to give Vice Admiral Lord Horatio Nelson the signal to stop the battle, Nelson chose to put his telescope before his blind eye and continue.

The burdens of the peasantry

'It was so beautiful out in the country,' writes Hans Christian Andersen – he was sitting with a view of a manor house park. The lords of the manor suffered no want, but life in the country was hard for those who were subject to drudgery and adscription. Adscription gave the lord of the manor the right to prevent tenured farmers between 4 and 40 years of age from moving from their place of birth. Drudgery meant that the tenured farmers were forced to work for the manor a certain number of days. During the 18th century this could mean as much as 265 days out of the year. The hard circumstances led to repeated peasant uprisings, though there is actually only one instance, where the tenured farmers killed their lord. The adscription was abolished in 1788, while the drudgery was phased out gradually. In the constitution of 1848 it became illegal to beat grown smallholders, or their wives. And with the co-operative movement the Danish farmers really took off.

KONGEN
BØD
STAVNSBAANDET
SKAL OPHØRE
LANDBOE LOVENE
GIVES
ORDEN OG KRAFT
AT
DEN FRIE BONDE
KAN VORDE
KIEK OG OPLYST
FLITTIG OG GOD
HÆDERLIG BORGER
LYKKELIG

The Liberty Memorial on Vesterbrogade by Copenhagen's main railway station was erected in 1792 in memory of the abolition of adscription. The four statues around the obelisk symbolize fidelity, diligence of the peasantry, valor, and civic virtues. On the monument is found the following inscription:
A just government which gives its citizenry liberty can expect the citizens to remain faithful to their country, work for the benefit of their fellow citizens, be encouraged toward diligence, a diligence which makes the country prosper, and that the citizen will be willing to defend his country.

Peasant family comes to town. A great exodus from country to town took place all around Denmark. The number of inhabitants in the capital and the chartered towns doubled during the years 1870 to 1890.

Child labor in the mid-19th century.

In the cobblestone streets

In the towns there was a great difference between rich and poor. If you were poor, you worked, even as a child. People without work begged, though this was outlawed by and by. But illness could hit rich as well as poor. The first instance of the Plague killed nearly half of Denmark's population, and several breakouts followed. After Cholera epidemic within the city walls of Copenhagen the first public housing was built in 1863. Brumleby, as this project is called is still a small oasis in the middle of the city. Inside the city walls the Copenhageners, rich and poor, were subjected to a hideous stench from the open sewers and outhouses during many centuries. Today the stench is gone, but the beautiful old neighborhoods are still there, both in Copenhagen and in a number of towns in the province, such as Køge and Ribe.

Emigration agent in Århus:
105 Dkr. to America.

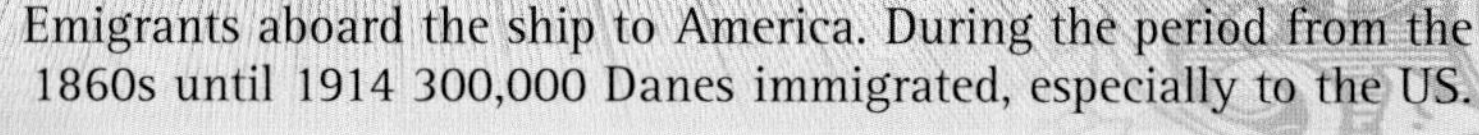

Emigrants aboard the ship to America. During the period from the 1860s until 1914 300,000 Danes immigrated, especially to the US.

Polish farm workers on Lolland. The great exodus created an increasing need for seasonal labor force. In 1930 the government put a stop to importation of Polish labor. This was not so much because of new technical achievements, but rather that hands were actually plentiful in Denmark.

Vesterbro around 1910.

Milkman's boys in Copenhagen.

Danish colonies

Denmark had colonies, both to the north, Iceland, Greenland, and the Faroe Islands, and more modestly in India and the West Indies. Copenhagen's trading monopoly for Greenland, Iceland, and the West Indies meant that the city could afford large palaces and castles during the 18th century. The tropical colonies in particular contributed to the prosperity. Denmark had two forts on the gold Coast from 1658, from where slaves were shipped to the three Danish West Indies Islands for the sugar cane production. Denmark did outlaw slave trading in 1803, but since slavery itself was not outlawed until 1848, this meant only that more emphasis was put on a 'domestic crop' than on transports from Africa. As the colonies grew increasingly unprofitable, they were sold or given away. After the first Danish public vote the three West Indies islands were sold to the US.

Polar bear hunt in Greenland.

Tranquebar, also known as Danish East India (today called Tarangambadi) was a Danish colony on the Indian south coast 1620-1845. In 1705 Frederik IV sent a German missionary to Tranquebar as a display of the Danish king's concern for the religious life of all his subjects. Christian VIII sold Tranquebar to the British in 1845.

Lunch at Christiansborg, Danish Guinea, in 1843. The governor, Edward Carstensen, standing in white, makes a toast to Prince Louis Philippe who, incidentally, painted this water color.

Saint Croix.

Slave at auction.

Dawn of the red flags

10
Socialdemokratisk Forening
10
FRIHED. LIGHED. BRODERSKAB
24. Januar
1895

Freedom, equality and brotherhood, a revolutionary slogan from the French revolution, was adopted by the labor movement. A poster from the Social Democrat Association.

The end of the 19th and beginning of the 20th century was characterized by social unrest and thoughts on democracy. Unemployment encouraged many to emigrate. During the 1880s about one in 10 Danes immigrated to America. New parties were formed, people read newspapers extensively, and thoughts of greater social equality became widespread. One of the many strikes of the day was about the abolition of the 11th work hour, the *slave hour.* Trade unions and employers' associations became stronger, women were allowed to vote, child labor was outlawed, and in 1915 the old constitution was renewed, so that more were allowed to vote. People receiving welfare however, were still not allowed to vote. After the war the old laws regarding servants were abolished, and an extensive social reform made it a right to receive public support.

Stauning
-eller Kaos
Stem
socialdemokratisk!

Tobacco worker Thorvald Stauning became the first worker to become prime minister in Denmark. During the 1930s he attained status of 'Father of the country', and he was respected far outside of Social Democrat circles. His portrait is known from the election poster from 1935 with the text *Stauning or Chaos*.

Children playing in a working class neighborhood.

The general strike of 1956. When the Social Democrat government in 1956 made into law a bargaining settlement which had been approved by the employers' association, but rejected by the labor unions, this resulted in a general strike. 200,000 workers gathered in front of Christiansborg, and on one sign it said:

Democracy
In Honor of thy Memory
The Workers of Tivoli

Denmark occupied

On the 9th of April 1940 Denmark woke up to the German occupation which was to last for five long years. In spite of the government's cooperation with the German occupation forces the population showed its disapproval with song meetings, demonstrations, general strikes, and sabotage, especially after the Germans had arrested the communists and detained the police. In a great coordinated effort 7,000 Danish Jews were sent to Sweden.

After the failure of the policy of collaboration execution of members of the resistance movement, and random gunning down of people in the streets became common fare. When the British bombed the Gestapo headquarters, the French girls' school unfortunately was also hit, and 112 died, primarily children. On the 4th of May Denmark was liberated – not Bornholm, however, which the Russians liberated a few days later. During most of the war Iceland and Greenland were occupied by the Americans.

Tens of thousands of Danish women had intimate relations with the soldiers of the occupational force, who left more than 5000 war children in their wake. After the war these women were humiliated and punished, here in Aalborg.

Soldier money.

The German soldiers called Denmark *The Whipping Cream Front.*

Horse power during the occupation.

The coastal defense ship Peder Skram was sunk by her own crew at Holmen on 29th of August 1943. It was raised by the Germans and hauled to Kiel, where it was rearmed with ant-aircraft guns and was made part of the German fleet under the new name of Adler.

The resistance movement at work at Kongens Nytorv.

Welfare society and youth revolt

Denmark's development into the current welfare society happened piecemeal after the war. The laws regarding old age pension took effect in 1958, the Social Security Act in 1976. During the late 1950s intense economic growth took off, people bought houses, got televisions, cars, etc. The young, however, turned against the suburban dreams of comfort, demonstrated against nuclear weapons and the Vietnam War, and established the free community of Christiania, while the women burned their bras and demanded equal wages. When Denmark legalized pornography, the country got a reputation for free-spiritedness and scantily clad blond girls. Nowadays, if you take a walk down Strøget, you will no longer see any naked people, but exciting shops, street musicians and crowds of Danes and tourists.

The 1980s were characterized by battles between the inhabitants and law enforcement. Now, who are the longhaired ones?

Happy Christmas! John Lennon, Yoko Ono and her little daughter in a Danish home in Thy.

Solvognen was an anarchist political theater troupe, in part with roots in the free community Christiania. On the 4th of July 1976 during the celebration of the 200th anniversary of the American Independence Day in Jutland, the theater troupe showed up as Indians on horseback at the top of the hills – just like in a real John Ford movie. On the other side of the valley were barefoot dancing Indians, while Greenlanders waved flags and banners together with Afro-Americans, Vietnamese and Cambodians.

A street scene from the free community Christiania. No to Hard Drugs is a slogan from the campaign instituted by the inhabitants against hard drugs which threatened the place during the 1980s.

Denmark and the world

After the Second World War little Denmark increasingly became an active participant in the larger world. Membership of NATO, The Nordic Council, passport freedom among the Nordic countries, membership in EFTA, later in EEC and EU. The Danes, however, are reluctant to embrace their membership in the European Union. The Euro has for instance not been adopted in Denmark, since the Danes voted against it in a special election. In 1979 a majority voted for Home Rule for Greenland in a special election. With the advent of charter tourism the Danes began traveling around the world in large numbers, and the World came to Denmark with fugitives and immigrants. Female succession was made possible in 1953, and the monarchy is alive and well.

The Danish soccer fans in Nyhavn.